SIGNS AND WONDERS

Encountering Jesus of Nazareth

A Catholic Guide for Small Groups

the
evangelical
catholic
forming disciples.
training leaders.

and

the WORD
among us®
press

Published by The Word Among Us Press
7115 Guilford Drive, Suite 100
Frederick, Maryland 21704
www.wau.org

20 19 18 17 16 1 2 3 4 5

Nihil obstat: The Reverend Michael Morgan, J.D., J.C.L.
Censor Librorum
July 6, 2016

Imprimatur: Most Reverend Felipe J. Estevez
Bishop of St. Augustine
July 6, 2016

ISBN: 978-1-59325-296-0
eISBN: 978-1-59325-486-5

Scripture texts are taken from the Catholic Edition of the Revised Standard Version Bible, © 1965, 1966 by the Division of Christian Education of the National Council of the Churches of Christ in the United States of America. Used with permission. All rights reserved.

Excerpts from the English translation of the *Catechism of the Catholic Church* for use in the United States of America ©1994, United States Catholic Conference, Inc.—Libreria Editrice Vaticana.

Cover design by Andrea Alvarez

Made and printed in the United States of America

Library of Congress Control Number: 2016943612

Contents

Introduction

Why Read about Jesus and His Followers?

How many times have you said to a friend something like this?

"You've just got to meet my friend _____! You would love him! He's so interesting! We enjoy lots of the same things, and we never run out of things to talk about. He's an awesome (skier, actor, basketball player, singer, or _____). Hey, we're getting together to hang out next Friday. Can you come too?"

Friends of a man named Jesus said very similar things about him almost two thousand years ago. What they said about Jesus was so important that they eventually wrote it down so that it would be remembered forever.

These stories about Jesus and his friends are in the four Gospels—found in the New Testament of the Bible. In this six-week guide, you can read about some of the most dramatic events in Jesus' life and discuss them using the questions provided or those you ask on your own.

Jesus taught with an authority that set him apart. His words had power and his touch could heal. Signs and wonders drew people to Jesus, both skeptics and believers. What Jesus said and did demanded a decision from them: who exactly was this Jesus? The answer to that question led some to walk away, but many others chose to follow him because *he changed their lives.*

These new believers shared with others the stories of Jesus, of how he had healed and freed them. Those people's lives were transformed too, and they told others; and so it continues to this day, to the ends of the earth.

You may not have yet decided what you think about Jesus. But whatever you think, it's clear that few figures in history have generated such far-reaching consequences for so long. Few cultures have been entirely shaped by one man in the way Jesus influenced the development of the Near East and the West.

If that intrigues you, then you might want to understand why he made such an impact. Reading the stories his friends left behind has helped people think about Jesus for the last two millennia. They will help you, too, to develop a sense of who he was, what he did, and what that could mean to you.

Even if it's just curiosity that's leading you to open this book and read this introduction, take the risk. Commit to attending a small group for all six sessions or to meditating on the readings and discussion questions by yourself. Either way, you will get to know Jesus.

No matter how you end up feeling about Jesus, after going through this guide, you will be more culturally literate and more aware of the big issues that engaged followers of this man and others for centuries. Plus, if you're in a small group, you'll be making friends with the other participants.

You already have something in common with your small group: you are all curious enough about Jesus to look a little deeper. You will probably find many other similarities as well. Make the commitment to become a community for these six weeks. Come to each meeting. Participate and be respectful of one another. Then watch as the riches unfold!

How to Use This Small Group Guide

Welcome to *Signs and Wonders*, a small group guide designed to help people know Jesus of Nazareth more deeply.

Weekly Sessions

In the weekly session materials, you will find opening and closing prayer suggestions, the Scripture passages to be discussed that week, questions for discussion, ideas for action, and prayer prompts to help you continue encountering Jesus through the week.

Unlike some small group Scripture discussion guides that progress consecutively through a book of the Bible, each session in this guide is self-contained. That way, if you or a friend attend a small group for the first time on Week 3, there won't be a need to "catch up"; anyone can just dive right in with the rest of the group. Instead of building sequentially, the sessions deepen thematically, helping you engage more with Jesus little by little.

The more you take notes, jot down ideas or questions, underline verses in your Bible (if you bring one to your small group), and refer back to previous sessions, the more God has the opportunity to speak to you through the discussion and the ideas he has placed in your heart. As with anything else, the more you put into it, the more you get back.

The best way to take advantage of each week's discussion is to carry the theme into your life by using the "Encountering Christ This Week" section. Your small group facilitator will talk about the recommendations during each session. You will have a chance to ask questions and share experiences from previous weeks.

If you're not in a small group, *Signs and Wonders* can be used on your own by considering the questions asked of each Scripture passage and following up with the suggestions in "Encountering Christ This Week."

Appendices

Helpful appendices for both participants and facilitators supplement the weekly materials. Appendices A through C are for participants, and Appendices D through F are for group facilitators.

Prior to your first group meeting, please read Appendix A, "Small Group Discussion Guide." These guidelines will help every person in the group set a respectful tone that creates the space for encountering Christ together.

This small group will differ from other discussion groups you may have experienced. Is it a lecture? No. A book club? No. Appendix A will help you understand what this small group is and how you can help seek a "Spirit-led" discussion. Every member is responsible for the quality of the group dynamics. This appendix will give you helpful tidbits for being a supportive and involved member of the group.

Appendix B is a resource to enhance and deepen your relationship with Jesus. In it you will find a step-by-step guide for reading Scripture on your own. It will show you how to meditate and apply what you find in Scripture. Appendix B also offers help in finding other spiritual reading that can increase your appreciation for the teachings and person of Jesus.

In Appendix C, you will find a guide to the Sacrament of Reconciliation. Commonly known as "Confession," the Sacrament of Reconciliation bridges the distance between God and us that can be caused by a variety of reasons, including unrepented sin. If you want to grow closer to Jesus and experience great peace, the

Sacrament of Reconciliation is an indispensable way to close the gap. This appendix leads you through the steps of preparing for and going to Confession in order to lessen the anxiety that you might feel.

While Appendices A through C are important for participants and facilitators alike, Appendices D through F assist the facilitator in his or her role.

A facilitator is not a teacher. His or her role is to support and encourage fruitful group discussion and tend to the group dynamics.

In Appendix D, the group facilitator will find guidance and best practices for facilitating a small group successfully. We've put together recommendations for dealing with problems in group dynamics that may come up. You will find guidelines on what makes a group work well: building genuine friendships, calling for the Holy Spirit to be the group's true facilitator, and seeking joy together.

Appendix E takes the facilitator from the general to the specific, providing detailed notes for each session in *Signs and Wonders*. Use this appendix as you prepare for each week's group meeting. The notes give the facilitator a heads-up on some of the content or context of the Scripture passage to be discussed that might be confusing or sufficiently important that he or she should draw attention to it. The notes also give tips on how to build group dynamics from week to week.

Appendix F helps the facilitator in leading prayer and encouraging participation in prayer by group members. While the material in each session includes a suggested prayer, Appendix F guides the facilitator in how to pray aloud extemporaneously and help others in the group to do so as well.

Learning this skill is important. It will model for the group members how to talk to Jesus in their own words. Closing with extemporaneous prayers is an extremely valuable way to honor the time the group has spent together by offering up the discoveries, questions, and joys of their conversation. Appendix F will help the facilitator guide the group from awkward beginnings to a deepening experience of talking to God.

Appendix F also gives the facilitator more information about how to use the "Encountering Christ This Week" section of each week's materials. The facilitator should encourage and support the group members in their personal engagement with that week's topic through their deepening commitment to allowing Jesus to become more and more a part of their lives.

Enjoy the adventure!

The Evangelical Catholic

week **1**

Wedding at Cana

"You have kept the
good wine until now."
—John 2:10

Praying together in your own words is always more natural than reading something together. Something simple and brief would be fine. You can ask the Lord's blessing on your time together or ask the Holy Spirit to guide your conversation, or you can just thank God for gathering you together to discuss the Scriptures. Begin and end the prayer with the Sign of the Cross, and you're ready to begin! If that feels too difficult, one person should slowly read the following prayer aloud, and invite the others to pray along silently in their hearts.

All | In the name of the Father, and of the Son, and of the Holy Spirit. **Amen.**

Reader | Heavenly Father,
Mary, the mother of Jesus,
spoke to her Son with confidence
in his power and his generosity.

May we courageously do the same
with our own needs,
especially with our need to notice
your presence in our lives.

We ask this in the name of Jesus,
your Son.

All | **Amen.**

Think back to the last wedding you attended. Which do you remember more, the vows and ritual or the party afterward? Why do you think those memories are the ones that stand out for you?

Ask one person to read the Scripture passage aloud.

John

¹On the third day there was a marriage at Cana in Galilee, and the mother of Jesus was there; ²Jesus also was invited to the marriage, with his disciples. ³When the wine failed, the mother of Jesus said to him, "They have no wine." ⁴And Jesus said to her, "O woman, what have you to do with me? My hour has not yet come." ⁵His mother said to the servants, "Do whatever he tells you." ⁶Now six stone jars were standing there, for the Jewish rites of purification, each holding twenty or thirty gallons. ⁷Jesus said to them,

2:1-11

"Fill the jars with water." And they filled them up to the brim. ⁸He said to them, "Now draw some out, and take it to the steward of the feast." So they took it. ⁹When the steward of the feast tasted the water now become wine, and did not know where it came from (though the servants who had drawn the water knew), the steward of the feast called the bridegroom ¹⁰and said to him, "Every man serves the good wine first; and when men have drunk freely, then the poor wine; but you have kept the good wine until now." ¹¹This, the first of his signs, Jesus did at Cana in Galilee, and manifested his glory; and his disciples believed in him.

1. Who are the main players in this narrative? What roles do they play?

2. How does Mary interact with Jesus? How do you think she feels about Jesus' response?

3. Based on this interaction, how might you describe their relationship?

4. What might Jesus be feeling when Mary makes her request?

5. What does Mary do after talking to Jesus? Why do you think she does this?

6. Do you think Jesus is being stingy in this story? Why or why not?

7. Why might Jesus have performed a miracle that only the servants witnessed? What might the servants have thought at each stage (hearing Mary's directions to them, following her directions, seeing the miracle)?

8. Does anything in this story cause you to think differently about your own relationship with Jesus? If you pray, does anything challenge you to pray differently?

9. This was the first of Jesus' miracles. It helped the disciples to believe he was something more than just another teacher or rabbi. In your life, can you think of anything you experienced as a sign that helped you to believe in Jesus?

Jesus' first public miracle was at a party, a wedding reception. At most weddings, joy flows! It probably did among Mary, Jesus, and the disciples too.

Have you ever been at a party when the refreshments ran short? What happened? Perhaps it embarrassed the host, but it also probably put a damper on the fun, causing people to leave early. Mary didn't want that to happen to her family or friends. She asked her son to solve the problem, even though he had never before done anything miraculous in public.

The life of discipleship certainly asks a lot of anyone who wishes to follow it, but it also promises real consolation and joy! The miracle at Cana makes it clear that Jesus wants joy to be part of his followers' lives.

Christians believe that joy comes from experiencing the love and presence of Jesus, who said, "I am with you always, to the close of the age" (Matthew 28:20). Followers of Jesus know this is true because we experience him with us every day. One of the hallmarks of beginning the Christian spiritual journey is an experience of joy that follows recognizing that God is active and present in our lives.

Even if you've never prayed before, take a moment this week to try talking to God about joy. What's the difference between happiness and joy? Do you have joy or happiness in your life? Have you ever had an experience of Christ's presence? Do you want one? Look back a bit over the past. Have you seen any small changes in yourself spiritually that carry a whiff of the joy of the miracle at Cana? Do you see a healthier, more joyful you emerging? If yes, celebrate that in some small way. If not, this week try asking Jesus, the source of joy, what stands between you and joy and what you can do about it.

Find a quiet place where you won't be interrupted, and talk to him as you would to anyone else. Formal prayers that don't expose your heart can resemble the kind of superficial conversation you might have with a stranger. Speak honestly and in your own words. Jesus wants you "in the rough" and "unvarnished." He wants you to talk to him about all your doubts, concerns, and dreams. He also wants you to be open to receiving whatever he wants to give you.

If you're a believer, try not to take for granted the free gifts God provides: life, health, home, family—whatever is true for you. This week, acknowledge, treasure, and savor the blessings in your life that often go unrecognized.

For Catholics, one of those blessings is the "new wine" at Mass in the Eucharist. This week consider going to Mass during the week. Watch for expressions of God's generosity in the prayers and rituals as you think about what the Eucharist is—the free gift of Jesus himself, who is truly present.

Have one person pray aloud while the others pray along silently.

All | In the name of the Father, and of the Son, and of the Holy Spirit. **Amen.**

Reader Christ Jesus,
We are astounded that we may come before
you to ask your help as we grow in our faith.

Faith is your gift.

It takes trust to ask you for an increase
in faith. Give us that kind of trust, Jesus.

Thank you, Lord, for being a generous giver!

We are excited that we can have an intimate
relationship with you.

We are grateful that we can begin a close
walk together.

Help us to have the same kind of trust in
you that your mother, Mary, had in asking
you for a miracle.

We ask you for the miracle of more faith
in our lives.

We ask for faith that helps us to believe that
you can answer our questions and solve our
problems, if we give you the chance.

We ask this in your name.

All | **Amen.**

week **2**

Walk on Water

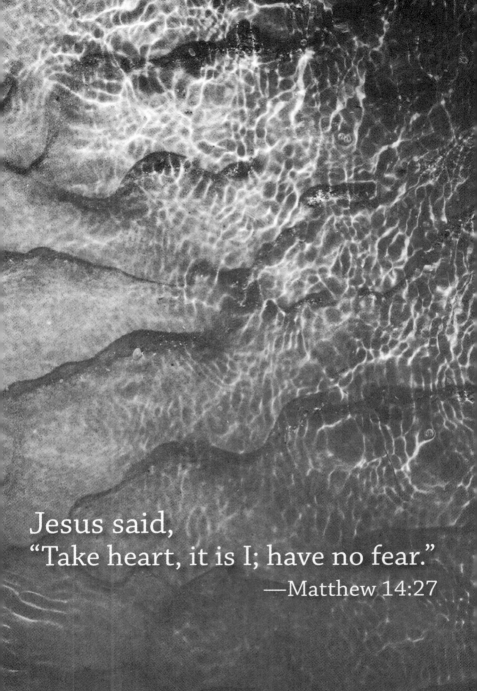

Jesus said,
"Take heart, it is I; have no fear."
—Matthew 14:27

Have one person read the prayer aloud while the others pray along silently.

All | In the name of the Father, and of the Son, and of the Holy Spirit. **Amen.**

Reader | Jesus,
You are God, and yet you became
human, like us.

You did not spare yourself the fear
and pain that we all sometimes feel.

You have shown us that our fear and
pain are not meaningless because you,
too, experienced it.

Now you walk beside us in our dark
moments.

Teach us how the fear and pain we un-
dergo can have meaning in you.

Help us to know that everything in our
lives can bring us closer to you.

We ask this in your holy name.

All | **Amen.**

Do you think that God is interested in you? In the details of your life? In the world? Have you ever doubted that God is even real? Do you think that the disciples ever had to deal with doubt of this kind?

Ask one person to read the Scripture passage aloud.

Matthew

²²Then he made the disciples get into the boat and go before him to the other side, while he dismissed the crowds. ²³And after he had dismissed the crowds, he went up into the hills by himself to pray. When evening came, he was there alone, ²⁴but the boat by this time was many furlongs distant from the land, beaten by the waves; for the wind was against them. ²⁵And in the fourth watch of the night he came to them, walking on the sea. ²⁶But when the disciples saw him walking on the sea, they were terrified, saying, "It is a ghost!" And they

14:22-33

cried out for fear. ²⁷But immediately he spoke to them, saying, "Take heart, it is I; have no fear." ²⁸And Peter answered him, "Lord, if it is you, bid me come to you on the water." ²⁹He said, "Come." So Peter got out of the boat and walked on the water and came to Jesus; ³⁰but when he saw the wind, he was afraid, and beginning to sink he cried out, "Lord, save me." ³¹Jesus immediately reached out his hand and caught him, saying to him, "O man of little faith, why did you doubt?" ³²And when they got into the boat, the wind ceased. ³³And those in the boat worshiped him, saying, "Truly you are the Son of God."

1. Why isn't Jesus in the boat along with his disciples?

2. What does Jesus do after the disciples leave? Why do you think Jesus does this before rejoining the disciples?

3. Describe the disciples' experience on the boat through verse 27.

4. What does Peter's request reveal about his personality? What does it indicate about his relationship with Jesus?

5. What do you think motivates Peter's desire to walk on water?

6. What might have gone through the other disciples' minds when Peter made this request of Jesus?

7. Why does Peter fall?

8. What could the boat symbolize? The crashing waves? What other symbolism do you see in this passage?

9. How does Jesus respond to the disciples' fear? How does he respond to Peter's fear?

10. Has the Lord ever saved you from sinking? What was that like?

11. Where is Jesus calling you to step out in faith? What is holding you back?

12. What does it mean to trust Jesus? How might trusting Jesus help you step out in faith instead of focusing on whatever strong winds buffet your life?

God's ways are mysterious. Jesus has come into the world and clarified many things about God that we couldn't have known otherwise, but not everything is crystal clear. God so values our free will that he will not force us to believe in him. He allows us to doubt or even reject him so that he will not overwhelm our free will.

Even if we pray regularly, we may sometimes wonder if there is anyone out there listening. Our understanding of God and his ways is limited and often distorted because we are both finite and, Christians believe, fallen. It can be hard to sense God or his leading in the midst of our daily circumstances.

God's silent presence in our prayer will always remain mysterious. And yet Jesus told us that he is always present and hears our every prayer. People who pray consistently often find that they have more peace during their day, even if they are bored and distracted most of their prayer time.

The Christian tradition teaches that when we make the choice to step out in faith, that act of trust and hope in the Lord brings tremendous blessing. Prayer is exactly that: trusting, or even just hoping, that God is there, no matter how obscure his presence may seem.

Jesus invites us to put all our faith in him, even when we don't understand how things could possibly work out for the best. A life of faith does not erase pain, doubt, or uncertainty, but it does change the way we respond to it.

This week, bring before the Lord a situation that concerns you. Imagine the Lord being with you in that situation. What is he saying to you? What is he doing? Imagine his calming power coming over this issue and coming over you. Imagine the Lord addressing you and asking you to trust in him. Speak to him as you would to your closest confidant, but with even more honesty, because you don't need to hold *anything* back. The practice of writing down your reflections and response to the Lord can be tremendously helpful. It gives God more ways to speak to you as you keep a record of your inner life.

Have one person read the prayer aloud while the others pray along silently.

All | In the name of the Father, and of the Son, and of the Holy Spirit. **Amen.**

Reader | Even when the emptiness of doubt dis-
turbs your soul, the Holy One is nurturing
within you a seed of faith.

Faith is the substance of what we hope for—
the evidence of what we cannot see.
(Hebrews 11:1)

Gracious God, there are times when my
ability to trust seems absent.

My heart longs for truth and I even find
within me a kernel of desire to believe, but
my mind seems unable to grasp the truth
and belief that I seek.

Let your sure and true presence wash over
me, shedding shafts of light where only
darkness resides,

and, in those shafts of light, may I see the
outline of your face.

I ask this for the sake of your love.

All | **Amen.**

—Renée Miller[1]

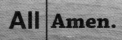

[1] Adapted from the website Explore Faith, accessed at http://www.explorefaith.org/
prayer/prayer/guided_prayer/prayer_for_when_youre_in_doubt.php

Jesus Raises a Girl from the Dead

Her spirit returned,
and she got up at once.

—Luke 8:55

Have one person read the prayer aloud while the others pray along silently.

All | In the name of the Father, and of the Son, and of the Holy Spirit. **Amen.**

Reader | Dear Lord of mercy and Father of comfort,

look upon me with eyes of mercy.

May your healing hand rest upon me,

May your lifegiving powers

flow into every cell of my body

and into the depths of my soul:

cleansing,

purifying,

restoring me to wholeness and strength

for service in your Kingdom.[1]

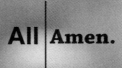

All | **Amen.**

[1] Adapted from the website Our Catholic Faith, "Healing Prayers," accessed at http://www.ourcatholicfaith.org/prayer/p-healing.html.

Do you believe that God is powerful, even though God doesn't always fix the problems in your life or in the world? Why or why not?

What would make you believe in God's absolute power over everything?

Ask one person to read the Scripture passage aloud.

Luke

---

⁴⁰Now when Jesus returned, the crowd welcomed him, for they were all waiting for him. ⁴¹And there came a man named Jairus, who was a ruler of the synagogue; and falling at Jesus' feet he besought him to come to his house, ⁴²for he had an only daughter, about twelve years of age, and she was dying.

As he went, the people pressed round him. ⁴³And a woman who had had a flow of blood for twelve years and had spent all her living upon physicians and could not be healed by any one ⁴⁴came up behind him, and touched the fringe of his garment; and immediately her flow of blood ceased. [45]And Jesus said, "Who was it that touched me?" When all denied it, Peter said, "Master, the multitudes surround you and press upon you!" [46]But Jesus said, "Some one touched me; for I perceive that power has gone forth from me." [47]And when the woman saw that she was not hidden, she came trembling, and falling down before him declared in the presence of all the people why she had touched him, and how she had been immediately healed. [48]And he said to her, "Daughter, your faith has made you well; go in peace."

8:40-56

[49]While he was still speaking, a man from the ruler's house came and said, "Your daughter is dead; do not trouble the Teacher any more." [50]But Jesus on hearing this answered him, "Do not fear; only believe, and she shall be well." [51]And when he came to the house, he permitted no one to enter with him, except Peter and John and James, and the father and mother of the child. [52]And all were weeping and bewailing her; but he said, "Do not weep; for she is not dead but sleeping." [53]And they laughed at him, knowing that she was dead. [54]But taking her by the hand he called, saying, "Child, arise." [55]And her spirit returned, and she got up at once; and he directed that something should be given her to eat. [56]And her parents were amazed; but he charged them to tell no one what had happened.

1. Could someone please summarize the events of this passage? What happens, step by step?

2. What do you think was the hemorrhaging woman's state of mind before her healing? What hints does the Scripture passage give about this?

3. What reason could Jesus have for insisting on knowing who had touched him (verse 45)?

4. How would you have reacted after being healed? How would you explain the woman's desire to remain hidden?

5. What might have gone through the woman's mind when Jesus called out, "Who touched me?" What do you think she was feeling as she finally came forward?

6. What might Jairus have felt as Jesus paused to care for this woman?

7. Jesus addressed the woman in verse 48 and Jairus in verse 50. What do these statements have in common?

8. How do you think Jairus felt when Jesus said, "Do not fear; only believe"? How would you feel in Jairus' circumstance?

9. Have you ever experienced a time when all seemed lost? Did anything help to strengthen your hope?

10. Are you tempted to be fearful about something in your life right now? How would you feel if Jesus said to you, "Do not fear; only believe"?

11. Take a moment of silence to imagine yourself as each of the different people in this story: Jairus, a member of his household, the mourners, the hemorrhaging woman, the crowds around Jesus, and the disciples. To whom do you most relate? Why?

The woman who touched the fringe of the Lord's garment was desperate enough to seek out Christ, compelled to touch him when it was clear that she would have no way to speak to him. Her action was even against the Mosaic law because she was ritually impure from her hemorrhage! Like Jairus, she had faith that brought forth Christ's power, a power that seemed to come so deeply from within Jesus that his mind was not even fully aware of how it happened. God's power and desire to heal us reside deep within his very being. He wants to heal us all the time.

Is there anything in your life that needs healing? Imagine Jesus surrounded by the pressing crowd. Imagine that you reach out to touch him, only to have him turn around and offer you time for conversation. Imagine that with the Lord you leave the crowd and find somewhere quiet so that you can talk to him.

He asks you to begin. Tell him everything you can about the healing and mercy you need. Let his compassion extend to you as his heart is moved with love for you.

Acknowledge this gift and let the Lord know of your gratitude. Let this gratitude flow over into worship of the great Healer, the divine Master—Jesus, the doctor of the sick and the friend to the sinner!

To experience Christ's presence more powerfully, try going to a weekday Mass. Listen for Jesus speaking to you through the readings. If a sentence, word, or image stands out for you, make note of it. God has drawn your attention to it for a reason. Ponder whatever you notice and talk to God about it. If you're Catholic, experience Jesus' love by spending some quiet time in prayer with him really and physically present in the Eucharist. If you are not Catholic, talk to Jesus about how he wants to give himself to you.

Have one person read the prayer aloud while the others pray along silently.

All | In the name of the Father, and of the Son, and of the Holy Spirit. **Amen.**

Reader | Father, you are great.
You are glorious.
You are holy.
You are loving, desiring good
for all your children.
Your greatness is larger than anything
we can understand.
You are the Lord of the heavens
and the earth,
Lord of nature and of humanity,
Lord of all creation.
All the earth is your handiwork.
And yet you draw near to us,
wanting to heal us,
to touch us, and to make us whole.
We fall at your feet, giving you thanks
for all you have done for us.
Help us to revere you in a way fitting
to who you are,
your power, your glory,
your supreme majesty,
and your steadfast love.

Jesus, we ask this in your holy name.

All | **Amen.**

week 4

Picking Wheat on the Sabbath

"I desire mercy,
and not sacrifice."
—Matthew 12:7

Have one person read the prayer aloud while the others pray along silently.

All | In the name of the Father, and of the Son, and of the Holy Spirit. **Amen.**

Reader Father, you know what is right and how you want us to act.

You know how best to reach us and steer us on a path of belief, love, and service.

Please remove the obstacles that prevent us from recognizing what is good and life-giving.

Jesus, help us to see our place in the world and to act along with you.

Please give us the confirmation we need so that we know we are on the right path.

Thank you for the good things you have promised us and have done so much to bring about.

Holy Spirit, open our hearts to your word, and help us to live from the riches you have placed within us.

Open our minds to reflect on ourselves, and prepare us for a deeper understanding of you.

Build us up as a community who seeks to know you and to walk in your ways.

We ask this through Christ our Lord.

All **Amen.**

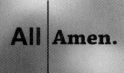

Have you ever been on a long hike without enough food, or have you ever been unable to get food for any reason when you were really hungry? If the opportunity presented itself, do you think you would have broken rules to feed yourself? For example, could you imagine picking fruit from someone's orchard without permission? Why or why not?

Ask one person to read the Scripture passage aloud.

Matthew

[1]At that time Jesus went through the grainfields on the sabbath; his disciples were hungry, and they began to pluck ears of grain and to eat. [2]But when the Pharisees saw it, they said to him, "Look, your disciples are doing what is not lawful to do on the sabbath." [3]He said to them, "Have you not read what David did, when he was hungry, and those who were with him: [4]how he entered the house of God and ate the bread of the Presence, which it was not lawful for him to eat nor for those who were with him, but only for the priests? [5]Or have you not read in the law how on the sabbath the priests in the temple profane the sabbath, and are guiltless? [6]I tell you, something

12:1-14

greater than the temple is here. [7]And if you had known what this means, 'I desire mercy, and not sacrifice,' you would not have condemned the guiltless. [8]For the Son of man is lord of the sabbath."

[9]And he went on from there, and entered their synagogue. [10]And behold, there was a man with a withered hand. And they asked him, "Is it lawful to heal on the sabbath?" so that they might accuse him. [11]He said to them, "What man of you, if he has one sheep and it falls into a pit on the sabbath, will not lay hold of it and lift it out? [12]Of how much more value is a man than a sheep! So it is lawful to do good on the sabbath." [13]Then he said to the man, "Stretch out your hand." And the man stretched it out, and it was restored, whole like the other. [14]But the Pharisees went out and took counsel against him, how to destroy him.

1. What are some activities and practices that Jews are traditionally forbidden to do on the Sabbath?

2. How would you describe the attitude of the Pharisees toward Jesus?

3. Why do you think Jesus refers to stories in the Old Testament?

4. What is Jesus trying to teach the Pharisees?

5. What claims does Jesus make about himself in this passage? What is your reaction to those claims?

6. Explain in your own words the meaning of Jesus' comparison of the value of a man to the value of a sheep.

7. Jesus quotes a teaching from the Hebrew Scriptures, "I desire mercy, and not sacrifice" (verse 7; cf. Hosea 6:6). What do you think he wants the Pharisees to understand? What is his criticism of them?

8. What are the ways in which you are tempted to think and act like the Pharisees? (For example, you might look down on people who go faster than the speed limit.) Where are you called to be more merciful to others?

9. Which Christian teachings sometimes cause people to begin to act like Pharisees? How do we find a balance between following Christian teachings and the spiritually dangerous possibility of behaving like a Pharisee?

As the Pharisees attempt to trip up Jesus and corner him in technicalities, Jesus stays true to his own profound knowledge of the ways of his Father. How can we develop such spiritual self-confidence and trust in God's character? One of the best ways is to ask Jesus to share some of his confidence with us during our times of prayer.

This week, find a quiet place, perhaps outdoors if the weather permits. Picture Jesus having returned to the wheat field once the Pharisees left the synagogue. What does the field look like? How large is it? Smell the air. What is the weather like? What is Jesus wearing? What are you wearing?

Then ask the Lord, "How do you keep your composure under pressure? Where does your trust in God, your Father, come from?"

Ask the Lord anything you want to know about his or your own relationship with the Father. Tell him what your experience with God has been, or what you have heard about God. Ask him anything you wish about your life or your knowledge of the ways of God. Imagine what Jesus would say or do in reply.

St. Ignatius of Loyola, founder of the Society of Jesus, taught that our imagination is one of the ways God communicates with us. We rarely hear an audible voice, but God uses all our faculties (imagination, memory, thinking, and reason) as natural means to talk with us. Ideas that startle us could be from the Lord!

If you desire a deeper and more trusting relationship with God the Father, ask Jesus in your own words to help you. Ask him to pray in you and with you. Then ask him to send you his Holy Spirit to stir up within you a longing for the life of freedom and confidence in the Father that he offers.

Have one person read the prayer
aloud while the others pray
along silently.

All | In the name of the Father,
and of the Son, and of the
Holy Spirit. **Amen.**

Reader Jesus, you told the Pharisees that "something greater than the temple is here" (Matthew 12:6).

We want that "something greater," Lord. We want you.

Please show us what our lives will be like if we entrust them to your Father.

May we experience the sweetness of your love and the greatness of your majesty so that we may be able to love our neighbors and ourselves.

Thank you for waiting so patiently for us to accept your love.

Help make us ready to take the next step in our relationship with you, Lord.

Please bless and guide us on the way.

We ask this in your holy name.

All | **Amen.**

week**5**

A Rich Young Man

"Come, follow me."
—Mark 10:21

Have one person read the prayer aloud while the others pray along silently.

All | In the name of the Father, and of the Son, and of the Holy Spirit. **Amen.**

Reader | Heavenly Father,
You are so high above us.

Sometimes we wonder if we will ever be able to live well in your ways, if we will ever have the courage to follow you to the end.

Hear us in our need, Lord. For without you and without the movement of your Holy Spirit, none of us would be able to follow you; none of us would be able to recognize you.

Assure us that we can approach you, Lord, and give us confidence that we can grow in the life you extend to us.

Be our comfort in the present and our perfection in the future.

We ask this in the name of your only Son, Jesus Christ our Lord.

All | **Amen.**

Do you think that valuing possessions or being acquisitive (wanting things) gets in the way of following Jesus? Why or why not?

Ask one person to read the Scripture passage aloud.

Mark

¹⁷And as he was setting out on his journey, a man ran up and knelt before him, and asked him, "Good Teacher, what must I do to inherit eternal life?" ¹⁸And Jesus said to him, "Why do you call me good? No one is good but God alone. ¹⁹You know the commandments: 'Do not kill, Do not commit adultery, Do not steal, Do not bear false witness, Do not defraud, Honor your father and mother.'" ²⁰And he said to him, "Teacher, all these I have observed from my youth." ²¹And Jesus looking upon him loved him, and said to him, "You lack one thing; go,

sell what you have, and give to the poor, and you will have treasure in heaven; and come, follow me." [22]At that saying his countenance fell, and he went away sorrowful; for he had great possessions.

[23]And Jesus looked around and said to his disciples, "How hard it will be for those who have riches to enter the kingdom of God!" [24]And the disciples were amazed at his words. But Jesus said to them again, "Children, how hard it is for those who trust in riches to enter the kingdom of God! [25]It is easier for a camel to go through the eye of a needle than for a rich man to enter the kingdom

10:17-31

of God." [26]And they were exceedingly astonished, and said to him, "Then who can be saved?" [27]Jesus looked at them and said, "With men it is impossible, but not with God; for all things are possible with God." [28]Peter began to say to him, "Lo, we have left everything and followed you." [29]Jesus said, "Truly, I say to you, there is no one who has left house or brothers or sisters or mother or father or children or lands, for my sake and for the gospel, [30]who will not receive a hundredfold now in this time, houses and brothers and sisters and mothers and children and lands, with persecutions, and in the age to come eternal life. [31]But many that are first will be last, and the last first."

1. What is the young man looking to learn from Jesus? How would you describe his attitude?

2. Which of the Ten Commandments does Jesus cite to the young man? Why do you think he chooses these?

3. What kind of life does the young man claim to have lived up to this point? Do you think the young man is being truthful?

4. Why do you think Jesus asks the rich young man to sell his possessions? Why would Mark include the detail that Jesus "looking upon him loved him" before Jesus makes this request? (verse 21).

5. How does the young man react to Jesus' invitation to follow him? How would you explain his reaction?

6. How do you think Jesus felt as the young man walked away?

7. When Peter asks, "Who can be saved?" (verse 26), what does Jesus say is necessary?

8. What do the young man and the disciples have in common? How are they different?

9. What statement does Jesus repeat in this passage? Why do you think he repeats himself?

10. How do you think Jesus wants us to view possessions? What might be preventing us from seeing what we own or what we want to own in his way?

11. What might Jesus be calling you to give up in order to follow him more closely? What would motivate you to do this? What keeps you from making the decision to give this to the Lord?

Jesus' response to the young man indicates that becoming his follower can be costly. We don't always feel peace and prosperity from the moment we decide to take Jesus seriously. To grow in the life he offers us, we need to count the cost of going deeper.

Though the journey asks much of us, we do not have to bear the burden alone. We can share our struggles with Christ in prayer, and we can seek prayer and support from our brothers and sisters in Christ.

Jesus will not always remove the burden from us, just as his Father did not remove the burden of the crucifixion from him in the Garden of Gethsemane. But he will always accompany us on the way, making our burdens easier to bear (Matthew 11:28-29). He will strengthen us (Isaiah 41:10). He will give us the peace beyond all understanding (Philippians 4:7) that makes our sacrifice possible.

Sit down and imagine the rich young man. Imagine that you are standing right behind him as Christ looks at him and speaks. When the rich young man leaves, Jesus wants to talk with you next. Share your thoughts and fears about what life with him could cost you. Let these thoughts and fears flow freely. Imagine Jesus answering you during this time of imaginative prayer. Do this throughout the week, listening for the movement of the Holy Spirit within your own spirit.

The Sacrament of Reconciliation provides an unparalleled opportunity to consider how you may be resisting Jesus. Many feel uneasy about partaking of this sacrament. Yet it offers a beautiful and consoling moment to honestly share our struggles and to hear Jesus' love and forgiveness through the priest's words and prayers. If you're Catholic, is the Holy Spirit prompting you to meet Jesus in the Sacrament of Reconciliation? Don't hesitate—go and experience God's mercy.

Appendix C includes a guide to the Sacrament of Reconciliation that will familiarize you with the sacrament before you go. But if the idea of going to Confession comes into your head when you're near a church, go whether you're prepared or not. That's a prompting from the Holy Spirit! Any priest will help guide you through Reconciliation should you want to receive this sacrament.

If you, like so many, feel uneasy about going to Confession, decide to talk to someone this week who goes to Confession regularly. Ask this person to share with you the role this spiritual practice plays in their life. Hearing about their experience may give you the courage and motivation to go yourself.

Have one person read the prayer aloud while the others pray along silently.

All | In the name of the Father, and of the Son, and of the Holy Spirit. **Amen.**

Reader Heavenly Father,
We need your grace to realize that we are
capable of changing in the ways you ask.

Inspire us, Lord, since nothing is
impossible with you.

We ask that you make us poor in spirit.

To be poor in spirit is to recognize our utter
and complete dependence on you and to say,
"Lord, I am nothing without you; I need you
desperately."

Help us to realize that being independent is a
virtue only in the eyes of the world. Show us
that in your kingdom, the more we are aware
of our need for you, O God, and our need for
one another, the more we will experience the
abundant life you came to bring us.

Through your Son, Father, make us poor in
spirit. Remind us that nothing is impossible
for you.

Bless us, O Lord our God.

All **Amen.**

week**6**

Doubting Thomas

"The disciples were glad
when they saw the Lord."

—John 20:20

Have one person read the prayer aloud while the others pray along silently.

All | In the name of the Father, and of the Son, and of the Holy Spirit. **Amen.**

Reader Lord,
Your life is so abundant that we
rejoice in your resurrection
even though we cannot
completely comprehend it.

Your power and majesty exceed
our ability to recognize you
as you are.

Jesus, prepare our hearts to
encounter you in your word.

Increase our faith, and help us
recognize the many ways
that you come to us.

Let us see in you, Jesus, how
we may best prepare for
our own meeting with you
face-to-face in glory.

All Amen.

Do the values or concerns of the world ever blind you to the goodness of God or discourage you from believing in God? How? What could you do to escape or counteract this discouragement?

John

[19]On the evening of that day, the first day of the week, the doors being shut where the disciples were, for fear of the Jews, Jesus came and stood among them and said to them, "Peace be with you." [20]When he had said this, he showed them his hands and his side. Then the disciples were glad when they saw the Lord. [21]Jesus said to them again, "Peace be with you. As the Father has sent me, even so I send you." [22]And when he had said this, he breathed on them, and said to them, "Receive the Holy Spirit. [23]If you forgive the sins of any, they are forgiven; if you retain the sins of any, they are retained."

[24]Now Thomas, one of the twelve, called the Twin, was not with them when Jesus came. [25]So the other disciples told him, "We have seen the Lord." But he said to them, "Unless I see in his hands the

20:19-31

print of the nails, and place my finger in the mark of the nails, and place my hand in his side, I will not believe."

[26]Eight days later, his disciples were again in the house, and Thomas was with them. The doors were shut, but Jesus came and stood among them, and said, "Peace be with you." [27]Then he said to Thomas, "Put your finger here, and see my hands; and put out your hand, and place it in my side; do not be faithless, but believing." [28]Thomas answered him, "My Lord and my God!" [29]Jesus said to him, "Have you believed because you have seen me? Blessed are those who have not seen and yet believe."

[30]Now Jesus did many other signs in the presence of the disciples, which are not written in this book; [31]but these are written that you may believe that Jesus is the Christ, the Son of God, and that believing you may have life in his name.

1. Why is the door locked? How does Jesus respond to his followers' feelings when he comes through the door?

2. In this passage, Jesus talks about forgiveness of sin (verse 23). How would you define sin?

3. How would you explain what Jesus is doing by giving the disciples the power to forgive and retain sins (verse 23)?

4. What sort of emotions might Thomas have felt when he heard the disciples claim to have seen Jesus? What would he have felt when he saw Jesus for himself?

5. This is often called the story of "Doubting Thomas." Do you think Thomas has a good reason for his doubts? Would the other disciples have believed if they had been in the same situation?

6. Why do you think the sight of Jesus' wounds is so important to Thomas and the other disciples?

7. Do you think Jesus holds Thomas' doubt against him? Why or why not?

8. What can you do to strengthen your faith when you're not sure if you really believe in God, or that Jesus was fully God and fully man?

9. Do you think it's okay to ask God for signs when you're unsure, or when you're looking for direction? Have you done this? What happened?

10. Do you think that seeking signs poses any spiritual dangers? If so, what would they be?

11. What does this story imply for us during times when we don't receive any sign, even when we feel we need one?

This week, find an opportunity to have a conversation with someone who has a strong faith. Try to meet this person for a meal or a cup of coffee so that you have the time to really talk.

If it feels natural, use the questions in this session as conversation starters. If not, discuss any questions or struggles you may have about believing in Jesus. If the person is Catholic, talk about the role of the sacraments in their relationship with God. What do they experience when going to Confession or celebrating the Eucharist?

How do they understand their Confirmation? How do they experience God in private prayer or Scripture reading? How do they handle feelings of doubt or disappointment or dryness in their relationship with God?

If you are comfortable, pray together about your struggles to believe. The Church brings us into a community, and we, as the body of Christ, the Church, depend upon one another to grow in faith. Together, ask for the intercession of St. Thomas as you continue on your path.

Have someone read the following aloud, or divide it up among the members of your group to read aloud. If time doesn't allow during a small group meeting, read later, or gather again for a final meeting to discuss. A final meeting on this material could be a great way to end your time as a group.

Becoming a person of faith isn't easy in our culture—it can feel entirely *counter*cultural. We are surrounded by doubters, agnostics, and those who tell us it is foolish to follow Christ. Belief in a Creator is often viewed as irrelevant and unscientific. Many scoff at the Christian moral code and decide to live by one of their own choosing. No wonder some seeking meaning and purpose in their lives would rather not look to Christ to find it! But goodness is a powerful draw, and Jesus' goodness is hard to deny, even for nonbelievers.

In the Gospel we last read, Thomas, a man who actually walked with Jesus before and after his crucifixion, has trouble understanding the ways of the Lord. How much more difficult it can be for those who have no interest in faith to comprehend God's ways! And yet our Lord wants to bring every skeptic to the fullness of faith, just as he did for Thomas. He wants to bring each of us to that fullness of faith too.

Think about the effect of these opposing forces on you, belief and skepticism, as you explore living your life in the Lord. Consider the ways of those who do not believe in Jesus and the ways of those who do. How does each group of people respond to the normal joys and struggles of daily life? How do

Christian believers and nonbelievers comprehend the meaning of life and death? Consider how you want to live. Discuss this together.

(Pause for discussion.)

Over the last six weeks we've talked about many aspects of human existence:

- the joy of celebration (Wedding at Cana—Week 1)
- the strong winds that buffet our lives, frightening us and derailing our efforts (Walking on Water—Week 2)
- our need for healing and hope (Jairus' Daughter—Week 3)
- a religious self-righteousness and closed-mindedness that condemn even good things (Picking Wheat on the Sabbath—Week 4)
- the power that possessions can have over us (Rich Young Man—Week 5)
- the struggle with doubt and the desire for a sign (Doubting Thomas—Week 6)

No matter who you are and what you believe, this is the stuff of life. A Christian isn't someone above or distant from struggling humanity. A Christian is a person deep in the midst of it, but different—different because he or she walks with Jesus, who came to be with us in our joys and sorrows.

Christians believe that Jesus came because God loves us and wants to be with us, now and always. This God, who is not some superpower in the sky but the One who loves each one of his children unconditionally as his own child, couldn't bear for us to remain distant from him. He doesn't want us ever far from what is real, in the darkness of eternal alienation.

You may have already made a decision about whether you want Jesus to be part of your life. You may not have. In either case, the way forward is to keep looking for Jesus. If you have decided for Jesus, then you already desire to understand him better and grow in relationship with him. If you haven't made a decision, the only way to continue exploring the question is to get to know him better.

We come to know people by hearing about them from others, talking to them ourselves, and spending intimate times with them. We get to know Jesus in the same way. We can learn of him in the stories his friends tell, "the great cloud of witnesses" (cf. Hebrews 12:1). These include friends you know now as well as the men and women of the ancient world in which Jesus lived, died, and rose. They so passionately wanted to share Jesus that they told and ultimately wrote down the stories of his life in what has become the Christian Scriptures.

The saints and great teachers often left written legacies of how they came to love Jesus and what he meant in their lives. Some witnessed to their love of Jesus by dying for him. For whom would you sacrifice your life? Your parents? Your children? Siblings? Friends? Strangers?

Jesus called his disciples friends, yet this is no ordinary friendship. It is a friendship that radically changes us. If you're still asking questions about Jesus, you need his friends, living and dead, to help you grow in understanding of the One who is not only friend but also teacher, brother, lover, savior, and Lord.

If you have friends who are also friends of Jesus, spending time with them or other Christians will help you continue to get to know Jesus better.

Getting to know him by reading Scripture and the writings of the saints requires commitment and sometimes some help. Appendix B in this booklet has a short guide on how to fruitfully read the Bible and spiritual writings. Start there. Commit time each day to prayerfully reading Scripture, reflecting, and seeking Jesus.

Another way to seek Jesus is at Mass. It's available to us every day of the week. If you're a Catholic, any growth that you have experienced in this small group will be intensified by frequently encountering Jesus sacramentally in the Eucharist. By wholeheartedly participating in the "source and summit"[1] of our faith, we open ourselves to understanding the fullness of who Jesus is and to living in his love more completely.

To "understand" someone means more than simply knowing that person. Knowing can mean mere acquaintance; understanding is much deeper. We can never completely figure out anyone, least of all Jesus, but "understanding" connotes far more than familiarity. If we understand a person, we have a feeling of profound empathy—a sense of that person's motivations as well as their hopes and dreams, hurts and fears, and mission and purpose.

Jesus can be understood—that's the good, the *great* news! Because he loves us, he desires to be known and understood as deeply as he knows and understands us.

Think of how much you want the people you love to understand you. How much more must Jesus want this, whose love and forgiveness of human failings are so great that he forgave the people who tortured and killed him *while they were doing it*.

Even if we don't think we want to know and understand Jesus, he is seeking us. Nothing can "separate us from the love of God in Christ Jesus" (Romans 8:39).

Seek the one who seeks you. You won't regret it.

---

[1]Documents of Vatican II, *Lumen Gentium*, 11; *Catechism of the Catholic Church*, 1324.

Have one person read the prayer aloud while the others pray along silently.

All | In the name of the Father, and of the Son, and of the Holy Spirit. **Amen.**

Reader | Lord Jesus, you are so generous with me, just as you were with the wine in Cana. You have loved me first and drawn me to you. Now I want to know you more and more.

In your goodness you created me for you; You placed within me a hunger for you that cannot be satisfied with the things of this world.

Lead me closer to you day by day: in prayer, in Scripture, in the sacraments, and in my daily life.

I want to treasure you above all things and always stay close to you.

Help me to love and adore you just as your mother, Mary, St. Thomas, and all the apostles adored you on earth, and as they do now in heaven.

All | **Amen.**

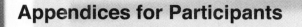

Appendices for Participants

(A) Small Group Discussion Guide

(B) A Guide to Reading Scripture, the Saints, and Spiritual Teachers

(C) A Guide to the Sacrament of Reconciliation

Appendix

A small group seeks to foster an honest exploration of Jesus Christ with one another. For many, this will be a new experience. You may be wondering what will take place. Will I fit in? Will I even want to come back?

Here are some expectations and values to help participants understand how small groups work as well as what makes them work and what doesn't. When a group meets for the first time, the facilitator may want to read the following aloud and discuss it to be sure people understand small group parameters.

Purpose

We gather as searchers. Our express purpose for being here is to explore together what it means to live the gospel of Jesus Christ in and through the Church.

Priority

In order to reap the full fruit of this personal and communal journey, each one of us will make participation in the weekly gatherings a priority.

Participation

We will strive to create an environment in which all are encouraged to share at their comfort level.

We will begin and end all sessions in prayer, exploring different ways to pray together over time. We will discuss a Scripture passage at every meeting. Participants do not need to read the passage beforehand—no one needs to know anything about the Bible in order to participate. The point is to discuss the text and see how it applies to our own lives.

Discussion Guidelines

The purpose of our gathering time is to share in "Spirit-filled" discussion. This type of dialogue occurs when the presence of the Holy Spirit is welcomed and encouraged by the nature and tenor of the discussion. To help this happen, we will observe the following guidelines:

- Participants strive always to be respectful, humble, open, and honest in listening and sharing: they don't interrupt, respond abruptly, condemn what another says, or even judge in their hearts.

- Participants share at the level that is comfortable for them personally.

- Silence is a vital part of the experience. Participants are given time to reflect before discussion begins. Keep in mind that a period of comfortable silence often occurs between individuals speaking.

- Participants are enthusiastically encouraged to share while at the same time exercising care to permit others (especially the quieter members) an opportunity to speak. Each participant should aim to maintain a balance: participating without dominating the conversation.

- Participants keep confidential anything personal that may be shared in the group.

- Perhaps most important, participants should cultivate attentiveness to the Holy Spirit's desire to be present in the time spent together. When the conversation seems to need help, ask for the Holy Spirit's intercession silently in your heart. When someone is speaking of something painful or difficult, pray that the Holy Spirit comforts that person. Pray for the Spirit to aid the group to respond sensitively and lovingly. If someone isn't participating, praying for that person during silence may be more helpful than a direct question. These are but a few examples of the ways in which each person might personally invoke the Holy Spirit.

Time

We meet weekly because that is the best way to become comfortable together, but we can schedule our meetings around any breaks or holidays when many people will be away.

It is important that our group start and end on time. Generally a group meets for about ninety minutes, with an additional thirty minutes or so afterward for refreshments. Agree on these times as a group and work to honor them.

Appendix  B

Once God gets our attention, we often find ourselves wanting more. Just as often, we don't have the first idea about how to seek God on our own without the support of our small group.

Catholic tradition contains a treasure trove of spiritual riches on which to draw. This appendix offers a variety of means by which to come to know Jesus more deeply: discussing Scripture with a friend, reading the Bible, and reading the writings of the saints and spiritual teachers. Skim to find what appeals to your heart.

For a Discussion with a Christian Friend
Please read Hebrews 4:12 together and discuss the following questions:

1. What does the metaphor "sharper than any two-edged sword" mean to you?

2. Why would the word of God penetrate "soul and spirit, joints and marrow"? What do you think the writer of Hebrews wants you to understand by this image/metaphor?

3. Can you explain in practical terms how the word of God judges the reflections and thoughts of the heart?

4. Have you ever experienced the word of God becoming "living" to you, touching your heart and mind to convert you, even if it was about something minor?

5. Do you ever turn to the word of God in times when you don't have anywhere else to turn? What have been the results?

6. What challenges have you had with Scripture? How have you been able to work through them?

Getting to Know Christ through the Bible

1. A pen and paper can make the difference between reading the Bible and really meditating on it—considering the story or teaching deeply in order to become more familiar with Jesus.

2. Write down observations about the text as you read and record questions that come to your mind, either in the margins of your Bible or in a journal.

3. Look up cross-references if your Bible has them, or look online, especially if they relate to your questions. Record your insights.

4. Find a key word in your text that interests you, and use an online concordance to review where else it appears. Read those other passages to deepen your understanding of the meaning of that word. Note your feelings.

5. For those who are more visual, draw a picture inspired by a Scripture story.

6. Summarize in writing what happened in the Scripture passage you read, or what the writer was saying.

The Three Essentials for a Rich Experience of God through Scripture: Memorize, Meditate, and Apply

Memorize

We may think that memorization is tedious and a waste of time, but that's not true. Having the words of Jesus or his followers readily at hand can be an important step in getting to know him. When you really come to know a friend, you will sometimes think, "I know what 'Joe' would say in this situation." This is also the case with Jesus. As you come to know him better, you'll want to be able to recall something he has said, because as you do, you will feel his presence more intensely. But you can only do this if you have memorized his words.

If you know it by heart, Scripture is available to you anytime, anywhere, day or night, whether you are free or imprisoned, healthy or sick, walking with a friend, or sitting quietly before the Eucharist.

Here are some techniques to help you with memorization:

1. Memorizing is much more fruitful after you've meditated on a passage. (See instructions for meditation below.)

2. Memorize steadily for a few days rather than cramming all at once. You will retain the information longer, and meditating on it will give you time to consider what is being said.

3. Continue to review the words you have memorized, or you will lose them. One of the best times to do this is right before you

fall asleep. At bedtime you don't need the fresh mind necessary for new memorization.

Meditate

Meditation is deep thinking on the teachings and spiritual realities in Scripture for the purposes of understanding, application, and prayer. A short description could be "absorption," "focused attention," or "intense consideration."

Meditation goes beyond hearing, reading, studying, or even memorizing. Instead, it is a means of absorbing the words and allowing God to speak to you through them.

Both Jews and Christians have attested that *God uses Scripture to speak to us.* When we make ourselves available to God mentally and spiritually in this way, he will reach us through his word.

God is gentle and gracious—he will never force us. Rather, he continuously invites us. When we give the time and attention that meditation requires, God in return gives us all the gifts a loving father longs to give his children.

Start with verses that conspicuously relate to your own concerns and personal needs. These can be found easily on any Internet search engine. (For example, search "Scripture passages on anxiety" or "Bible verses on seeking God's strength.") Through Scripture passages relevant to your life, God can meet your needs very quickly. He wants our communication with Jesus to be rooted in his word.

Some tips and methods for meditation:

1. Summarize in your own words what the passage is saying, or what happens in what order in a narrative or dialogue.

- You can do this in your head, but it's even better if you jot it down in a journal. This is an extremely useful practice. Some of us think we know the Scriptures because they are proclaimed in church, particularly the Gospels. When we try to summarize in the order of events/dialogue, however, we learn how much we have been missing!

- Don't worry about trying to summarize from memory—you should go back to the text to clarify. Sometimes observing that you have glossed over verses can be an indication that you need to spend time on a particular teaching.

2. Talk to Jesus about the Scripture passage you are reading.

- By talking to Jesus, you submit your mind to the Holy Spirit's illumination of the text and intensify your spiritual perception.

- Allow time for both reading and talking to Jesus. If you rush through the reading, you won't retain anything. If you say a few words to Jesus and then dash off, you aren't really giving him time to speak or explain things to you. Think how much you retain or receive when you're rushed in speaking to another person. It's the same with God!

3. Don't bite off more than you can chew. Better to read and consider a few verses or a short passage than to ingest big chunks without meditation.

Apply

If we do something about what we have read, what we read is incorporated into our lives as it can be in no other way. "Be doers of the word, and not hearers only, deceiving yourselves" (James 1:22). An application is a concrete step you can take in response to your prayer and meditation.

1. Expect to find an application—open the Bible in anticipation of discovering what you need!

2. Meditate to discern an application. Meditation isn't an end in itself. It leads to inner transformation, and inner transformation comes from and leads to action.

3. Sometimes an action step is so evident that it jumps off the page. If this doesn't happen, be sure to ask questions of the text that orient you towards action. For example:

- Does this text reveal something I should believe?

- Does this text reveal something I should praise or thank or trust God for?

- Does this text reveal something I should pray about for myself and others?

- Does this text reveal something about which I should have a new attitude?

- Does this text reveal something about which I should make a decision?

- Does this text reveal something I should do for the sake of Christ and others or myself?

Commit to one specific response. Less is more if you really do it.

Scripture reading and meditation techniques are necessary because we all need to prevent shallow reading. Modern technology forms us for fast and superficial communication. In fact, we often talk to others shallowly because our attention is on texting, tweeting, the next thing we're doing—the list is endless!

We must fight this tendency for the sake of our humanity. In one episode of an old sci-fi television show, the original *Star Trek*, the former inhabitants of another planet had continually sped up, ultimately moving so fast that they became merely buzzing sounds. When they invaded the starship *Enterprise*, the crew thought that flies had come in with the food supplies. These aliens had lost their very beings because they valued speed above all else.

Watch to see if you're reading Scripture hurriedly or in a perfunctory way because you think you should, not because you are seeking to meet God there.

If Jesus met you on the street today, do you think he would be shallow, half listening, rushed, or distracted? Can these be the ways of a loving God? If not, then they can't be the way of a loving person either! Remember, Christ is those "other people" you will meet on the street and everywhere you go each day. Loving attention to God in Scripture forms us for loving attention to others.

Spiritual Reading

The Church has consistently valued the witness of the communion of saints. We are fortunate that as Catholics, we have a rich tradition of stories of holy men and women whose lives have witnessed to their great love of God and others. In addition, many saints canonized by the Church, as well as other spiritual teachers, have left written or artistic works that the Church recognizes as invaluable tools for coming to know God.

Perhaps—especially if you were raised Catholic—you already have an interest in a specific saint or spiritual teacher. If so, find out if that saint has left any written or artistic works. Either can be used to consider Jesus. Or ask a friend about saints whose writings have helped them. Biographies of the lives of saints and Christian heroes can also be inspiring reading.

Spiritual reading is much like Scripture meditation. If we read quickly and do not consider what we have read, nothing much sticks. If we read slowly and allow time to think about what we have read, then we absorb it. God communicates with us through considered reading.

Scripture reading with meditation holds priority over spiritual reading because Christians have always taught that the Scriptures are the privileged means by which God works in our hearts and minds. That is why Christians encourage daily reading of Scripture above any other spiritual reading. The saints and spiritual teachers enlighten and inspire us for the reading of Scripture.

The Evangelical Catholic recommends reading and meditating on Scripture in the morning, when you are fresh, or during a break in your day. You can save the spiritual reading for later on, either in the evening or at bedtime.

Writings of the Saints and Christian Teachers

Some classics that have helped those seeking to know Christ:

The Way of Perfection by Teresa of Avila. This is the best book to begin with when reading St. Teresa. A Doctor of the Church, Teresa is loved by many for her writings on prayer and the spiritual life. This book is short and simple. Teresa's direct language and folksy style make for a particularly engaging read.

Autobiography of Teresa of Avila, also called *The Story of Her Life.* This is longer than *The Way of Perfection* and includes St. Teresa's famous metaphor on prayer as a garden. Read this when you're ready for extended time with St. Teresa.

The Story of a Soul, also called *The Autobiography of St. Thérèse of Lisieux.* In surveys on favorite saints, St. Thérèse consistently tops the list. She speaks in her memoir with an unaffected, honest voice, almost like the voice of a child. She died as a cloistered Carmelite nun at the age of twenty-four, but despite her young age, she was soon recognized as a spiritual giant. St. Thérèse is known for her "little way" of humble love. For first-time readers, her little way may appear simple or silly. But once you try it, you learn that loving sacrificially, like Jesus, truly does require you to lose your life in order to save it.

Introduction to the Devout Life by St. Francis de Sales. This is a great read for beginners because it has so much direction on how to live as a follower of Jesus. You can read each short and accessible chapter in only ten to fifteen minutes. Reading one each day will give you plenty of real spiritual meat to chew on.

Pensées by Blaise Pascal. This classic has influenced countless Christians. Pascal was a seventeenth-century mathematician. The *pensées*, or "thoughts," are scattered fragments of his theological and philosophical ponderings after his conversion to Christianity.

New Seeds of Contemplation and *No Man Is an Island* by Thomas Merton. Merton is widely considered one of the greatest spiritual writers of the twentieth century. His compartmentalized prose provides quick, sophisticated reading "nuggets" capable of leading you into profound thoughts on God. The language of his later works is more accessible than those of his earlier ones.

The Confessions of Saint Augustine. This well-loved classic details Augustine's search for God. The immediacy of his struggle to believe is evident and something every person, even today, can relate to. Augustine's conversion story finishes with Book 9. The later chapters are written as a long disquisition on time and memory. This is rich stuff, but it's not for every reader.

The Imitation of Christ by Thomas à Kempis. Apart from the Bible, no book has been translated into more languages than this classic. It was a favorite of Teresa of Avila, Thomas More, Ignatius of Loyola (founder of the Jesuits), Thérèse of Lisieux, and countless saints and Christians of other denominations, including John Wesley and John Newton, founders of the Methodist movement. The book has remained popular because of its profound insights about human nature and the struggle to live a holy life.

Autobiography of Saint Ignatius of Loyola. This short description of St. Ignatius' famous conversion from a womanizing soldier to a Christian mendicant, or beggar, is both a classic and an easy read. The story includes Ignatius' observations on his interior life while convalescing from serious war wounds. These become not only the immediate cause of his conversion but also the groundwork for his thought on the discernment of spirits in his *Spiritual Exercises.*

The Long Loneliness by Dorothy Day. Day was a worldly young communist in New York City in the heyday of early twentieth-century social movements. She lived as many young women live today: taking lovers, having an abortion, and promoting a secular salvation through political change. After her conversion to Catholicism, Day founded the Catholic Worker movement, still in existence today, to offer hospitality to Christ in the poor and needy. Simply written and very moving, Day's is one of the great conversion stories of the last century.

Appendix

If it has been a long time since you last went to Confession—or if you've never been—you may be hesitant and unsure. Don't let these very common feelings get in your way. Reconciling with God and the Church always brings great joy. Take the plunge—you will be glad you did!

If it will help to alleviate your fears, familiarize yourself with the step-by-step description of the process below. Most priests are happy to help anyone willing to take the risk. If you forget anything, the priest will remind you. So don't worry about committing every step and word to memory. Remember, Jesus isn't giving you a test; he just wants you to experience the grace of his mercy!

Catholics believe that the priest acts *in persona Christi*, "in the person of Christ." The beauty of the sacraments is that they touch us both physically and spiritually. On the physical level in Confession, we hear the words of absolution through the person of the priest. On the spiritual level, we know that it is Christ assuring us that he has truly forgiven us. We are made clean!

You usually have the option of going to Confession anonymously—in a confessional booth or in a room with a screen—or face-to-face with the priest. Whatever your preference will be fine with the priest.

Steps in the Sacrament of Reconciliation:

1. Prepare to receive the sacrament by praying and examining your conscience. If you need help, you can

find many different lists of questions online that will help you examine your conscience.

2. Once you're with the priest, begin by making the Sign of the Cross while greeting the priest with these words: "Bless me, Father, for I have sinned." Then tell him how long it has been since your last confession. If it's your first confession, tell him so.

3. Confess your sins to the priest. If you are unsure about anything, ask him to help you. Place your trust in God, who is a merciful and loving Father.

4. When you are finished, indicate this by saying, "I am sorry for these and all of my sins." Don't worry later that you forgot something. This closing statement covers everything that didn't come to mind in the moment. Trust God that he has brought to mind what he wants you to address.

5. The priest will assign you a penance, such as a prayer, a Scripture reading, or a work of mercy, service, or sacrifice.

6. Express sorrow for your sins by saying an Act of Contrition. Many versions of this prayer can be found online. If memorization is difficult for you, just say you're sorry in your own words.

7. The priest, acting in the person of Christ, will absolve you of your sins with prayerful words, ending with "I absolve you from your sins in the name of the Father, and of the Son, and of the Holy Spirit." You respond by making the Sign of the Cross and saying, "Amen."

8. The priest will offer some proclamation of praise, such as "Give thanks to the Lord, for he is good" (from Psalm 136). You can respond, "His mercy endures forever."

9. The priest will dismiss you.

10. Be sure to complete your assigned penance immediately or as soon as possible.

Appendices for Facilitators

D The Role of the Facilitator

E A Guide for Each Session of *Signs and Wonders*

F Leading Prayer and "Encountering Christ This Week"

Appendix

Perhaps no skill is more important to the success of a small group than the ability to facilitate a discussion lovingly. It is God's Holy Spirit working through our personal spiritual journey, not necessarily our theological knowledge, that makes this possible.

The following guidelines can help facilitators avoid some of the common pitfalls of small group discussion. The goal is to open the door for the Spirit to take the lead and guide your every response because you are attuned to his movements.

Pray daily and before your small group meeting. This is the only way you can learn to sense the Spirit's gentle promptings when they come!

You Are a Facilitator, Not a Teacher

As a facilitator, it can be extremely tempting to answer every question. You may have excellent answers and be excited about sharing them with your brothers and sisters in Christ. However, a more Socratic method, by which you attempt to draw answers from participants, is much more fruitful for everyone else and for you as well.

Get in the habit of reflecting participants' questions or comments to the whole group before offering your own input. It is not necessary for you as a facilitator to enter immediately into the discussion or to offer a magisterial answer. When others have sufficiently addressed an issue, try to exercise restraint in your comments. Simply affirm what has been said; then thank them and move on.

If you don't know the answer to a question, have a participant look it up in the *Catechism of the Catholic Church* and read it aloud to the group. If you cannot find an answer, ask someone to research the question for the next session. Never feel embarrassed to say, "I don't know." Simply acknowledge the quality of the question and offer to follow up with that person after you have done some digging. Remember, you are a facilitator, not a teacher.

Affirm and Encourage

We are more likely to repeat a behavior when it is openly encouraged. If you want more active participation and sharing, give positive affirmation to the responses of the group members. This is especially important if people are sharing from their hearts. A simple "Thank you for sharing that" can go a long way in encouraging further discussion in your small group.

If someone has offered a theologically questionable response, don't be nervous or combative. Wait until others have offered their input. It is very likely that someone will proffer a more helpful response, which you can affirm by saying something such as "That is the Christian perspective on that topic. Thank you."

If no acceptable response is given and you know the answer, exercise great care and respect in your comments so as not to appear smug or self-righteous. You might begin with something such as "Those are all interesting perspectives. What the Church has said about this is . . . "

Avoid Unhelpful Tangents

Nothing can derail a Spirit-filled discussion more quickly than digressing on unnecessary tangents. Try to keep the session on track. If conversation strays from the topic, ask yourself, "Is this a

Spirit-guided tangent?" Ask the Holy Spirit too! If not, bring the group back by asking a question that steers conversation to the Scripture passage or to a question you have been discussing. You may even suggest kindly, "Have we gotten a little off topic?" Most participants will respond positively and get back on track through your sensitive leading.

That being said, some tangents may be worth pursuing if you sense a movement of the Spirit. It may be exactly where God wants to steer the discussion. You will find that taking risks can yield some beautiful results.

Don't Fear the Silence

Be okay with silence. Most people need a moment or two to come up with a response to a question. People naturally require some time to formulate their thoughts and put them into words. Some may need a few moments just to gather the courage to speak at all.

Regardless of the reason, don't be afraid of a brief moment of silence after asking a question. Let everyone in the group know early on that silence is an integral part of normal small group discussion. They needn't be anxious or uncomfortable when it happens. God works in silence!

This applies to times of prayer as well. If no one shares or prays after a sufficient amount of time, just move on gracefully.

The Power of Hospitality

A little hospitality can go far in creating community. Everyone likes to feel cared for. This is especially true in a small group whose purpose it is to connect to Jesus Christ, a model for care, support, and compassion.

Make a point to greet people personally when they first arrive. Ask them how their day has been going. Take some time to invest in the lives of your small group participants. Pay particular attention to newcomers. Work at remembering each person's name. Help everyone feel comfortable and at home. Allow your small group to be an environment in which authentic relationships take shape and blossom.

Encourage Participation

Help everyone to get involved, especially those who are naturally less vocal or outgoing. To encourage participation initially, always invite various group members to read aloud the selected readings. Down the road, even after the majority of the group feels comfortable sharing, you may still have some quieter members who rarely volunteer a response to a question but would be happy to read.

Meteorology?

Keep an eye on the "Holy Spirit barometer." Is the discussion pleasing to the Holy Spirit? Is this conversation leading participants to a deeper personal connection to Jesus Christ? The intellectual aspects of our faith are certainly important to discuss, but conversation can sometimes degenerate into an unedifying showcase of intellect and ego. Other times discussion becomes an opportunity for gossip, detraction, complaining, or even slander. When this happens, you can almost feel the Holy Spirit leaving the room!

If you are aware that this dynamic has taken over a discussion, take a moment to pray quietly in your heart. Ask the Holy Spirit to help you bring the conversation to a more wholesome topic. This can often be achieved simply by moving to the next question.

Pace

Generally, you want to pace the session to finish in the allotted time, but sometimes this may be impossible without sacrificing quality discussion. If you reach the end of your meeting and find that you have covered only half the material, don't fret! This is often the result of lively Spirit-filled discussion and meaningful theological reflection.

In such a case, you may take time at another meeting to cover the remainder of the material. If you have only a small portion left, you can ask participants to pray through these on their own and come to the following meeting with any questions or insights they may have. Even if you must skip a section to end on time, make sure you leave adequate time for prayer and to review the "Encounter Christ This Week" section. This is vital in helping participants integrate their discoveries from the group into their daily lives.

Genuine Friendships

The best way to show Jesus' love and interest in your small group members is to meet with them for coffee, dessert, or a meal outside of your small group time.

You can begin by suggesting that the whole group get together for ice cream or some other social event at a different time than when your group usually meets. Socializing will allow relationships to develop. It provides the opportunity for different kinds of conversations than small group sessions allow. You will notice an immediate difference in the quality of community in your small group at the next meeting.

After that first group social, try to meet one-on-one with each person in your small group. This allows for more indepth conversation and personal sharing, giving you the chance to know each participant better so that you can love and care for them as Jesus would.

Jesus called the twelve apostles in order that they could "be with him" (Mark 3:14). When people spend time together, eat together, laugh together, cry together, and talk about what matters to them, intense Christian community develops. That is the kind of community Jesus was trying to create, and that must be the kind of community we try to create, because it changes lives. And changed lives change the world!

Joy

Remember that seeking the face of the Lord brings joy! Nothing is more fulfilling, more illuminating, and more beautiful than fostering a deep and enduring relationship with Jesus Christ. Embrace your participants and the entire spiritual journey with a spirit of joyful anticipation of what God wants to accomplish.

"These things I have spoken to you, that my joy may be in you, and that your joy may be full." (John 15:11)

Appendix (E)

God can respond to us personally through the Scriptures, no matter how much knowledge we have of biblical times. But God can also speak to us through commonly known information about the social and religious situations at the time in which Jesus lived. These notes will help you assist your group to better understand the Scriptures you read each week.

While some of these historical and religious facts are fascinating, always resist any urge to teach too much rather than facilitate a conversation. This information is provided in case the conversation goes in a direction in which knowing these facts would be relevant and helpful. In that case, share briefly—ideally in your own words—and then ask a question about how this can deepen their understanding of what was happening. In other words, give the conversation back to the group as quickly as possible.

The notes for Week 1 include suggestions on ways to make people feel comfortable, while the notes for Week 6 provide ideas for encouraging participants to go forward in a deepening life in Christ.

Review the notes for each session as you prepare each week. Jot notes so you can summarize the information provided in your own words should it be relevant to the conversation.

Week 1
Wedding at Cana

Everyone in your small group may not know one another. So the first time you meet, you can set people at ease by asking a few questions. You can use the ones we have suggested below, or you can formulate your own.

In choosing questions, it's important that they have no right or wrong answer; choose topics about which no one could feel that their answer is the only right one. Be sure to avoid anything controversial. During this process, you can ask people to share their names.

- Who is the greatest quarterback in the NFL?

- What do you think is the best way to spend a vacation?

Here are some examples of responses:

- "I'm Greg. I'm a freshman in _____ dorm and a friend of _____. He made me come! I think that Peyton Manning is the greatest quarterback the NFL has ever seen or ever will!"

- "I'm Leslie, mother of three and a parishioner at St. Luke's. The best way I could spend a vacation is to have a full-time nanny for a week—anywhere."

Scripture Discussion

If the discussion turns to the significance of the shortage of wine at the wedding, it may be helpful to explain the importance of wine in the time of Jesus. Wine was especially associated with dining, feasts, and celebrations.[1] Because of its connotations of blessing, joy, and abundance, wine being absent at a wedding celebration would particularly embarrass a host.

If the large water jars become relevant to the discussion, it may be helpful to share that these were likely present for the use of Jewish ritual washings. Washing was part of the law that guided every observant Jew's life.

Your group could explore the symbolism of Jesus replacing the water for purification with wine, but don't force this if it doesn't come up in the conversation. According to one Scripture scholar, "This replacement is a sign of who Jesus is, namely, the one sent by the Father who is now the only way to the Father. All previous religious institutions, customs and feasts lose meaning in his presence."[2] The main point is this: the same Jesus who changed water into wine can also transform us.

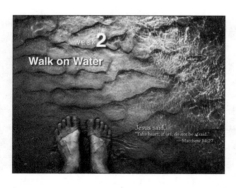

Jesus said,
"Take heart, it is I; do not be afraid."
—Matthew 14:27

Week 2
Walk on Water

The "Encountering Christ This Week" section focuses on God's loving presence with us through all trials, hardships, and doubts. When we say that God "allows us to doubt or even

---

[1] "Wine." *HarperCollins Bible Dictionary,* © 2015, Society of Biblical Literature. Online at Bible Odyssey, http://www.bibleodyssey.org/HarperCollinsBibleDictionary/w/wine.aspx.

[2] Raymond E. Brown, SS, *The Anchor Bible: The Gospel According to John (I-XII)* (New York: Doubleday, 1966), p. 104.

reject him so that he will not overwhelm our free will," or that "God's ways are mysterious," we do not at all mean that God actively prevents us from believing in him. Rather, he leaves it up to us to choose to believe in him. An overwhelming display of his power might prevent us from freely choosing him. By his constant and often silent presence, we are invited to a deeper level of trust and abandonment to his love and care.

Be careful not to allow the discussion to become heavily focused on doubt or free will. Discussion of philosophical ideas can quickly derail Spirit-filled sharing. If the subject comes up, invite the group members to share their personal struggles of prayer and of trusting in Jesus. Remind them of the themes and applications you explored during your discussion of Peter walking on water. Jesus' invitation to step out of the boat could be a useful theme to draw people back to sharing about their spiritual lives rather than exploring concepts and theories.

As a general rule, always draw a heavy philosophical discussion back to Jesus' invitation for each person to encounter him personally. By redirecting the discussion, you will encourage participants to take their hearts and experiences humbly to God himself. Ultimately, it is Jesus who will give them the grace to consider the intellectual issues in light of faith and to persevere through any and every hardship in their lives.

However, don't ignore the thoughts and ideas of your group members. If someone is struggling more deeply and intensely with doubts about God, or has a question about free will, it is usually not helpful to address it in the group time. Try to meet with that person one-on-one to talk further. That is a better way to support and encourage someone in their specific situation and to address their concerns.

As group members converse about any philosophical topic, never cut off anyone who is sharing intellectual concerns. Instead, affirm him or her, say that you would love to hear more or explore their thoughts further outside of the group, and gently direct the conversation back to a discussion in which all group members can participate.

Encourage all group members to pray for one another to experience a life-giving encounter with Jesus that will help them believe or strengthen their faith. Remind them of Jesus' words to the disciples in the boat: "Take heart, it is I; have no fear" (Matthew 14:27). It is in these times of doubt, when we cry out to the Lord, "Save me," that Jesus takes us by the hand, like Peter, and catches us. That's when we can abandon doubt and put our faith in Jesus.

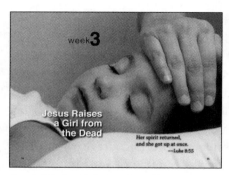

Week 3
Jesus Raises a Girl from the Dead

This week's Scripture passage retells two miracles: Jesus heals the hemorrhaging woman and raises Jairus' daughter from the dead. Both of these situations appeared to be hopeless. The woman had bled for twelve years (perhaps signifying permanence), and the little girl was dead. Both of them were ritually unclean.

The Torah (the first five books of the Old Testament) contains hundreds of laws for Israel regarding ritual purity. The woman with the flow of blood is subject to one of these laws: "According to Leviticus 15:25-31, such a woman would be 'unclean' and had to be separated from Israel."[3] Anything or anyone she touched would have become unclean, requiring ritual washing and a period of purification. Likewise, anyone touching a dead body would become unclean as well (Numbers 19:11-12).

[3] Joseph A. Fitzmyer, SJ, *The Anchor Bible: The Gospel According to Luke (I-IX)* (New York: Doubleday, 1981), p. 746.

Through these two miracles, Jesus demonstrated that God can do the impossible and that God's love can overcome all barriers. This should give your group members confidence to bring their impossible situations to God in prayer.

If it becomes relevant to the discussion, your group might explore the significance of the woman coming out in public and the implications of her touching Jesus. Ask participants what that might mean for their own lives. How might they reach out to Jesus in faith?

For question 11, be sure to allow a good full minute of silence. It may seem like a long time, but that is because you, as the group facilitator, have already thought about the question. It will take a while for everyone in your group to imagine themselves as the different characters. Always be comfortable with the silence—God works in it!

Week 4
Picking Wheat on the Sabbath

Not everyone in your small group may know exactly who the Pharisees were. According to the Jewish historian Josephus, the Pharisees were an influential group considered to be authoritative interpreters of Jewish law who also zealously observed it, especially laws concerning the Sabbath.[4]

In rabbinical texts, many kinds of work are declared forbidden on the Sabbath, including reaping, yet the rabbis allowed the

[4] "Pharisees." *HarperCollins Bible Dictionary,* © 2015, Society of Biblical Literature. Online at Bible Odyssey, http://www.bibleodyssey.org/people/main-articles/pharisees.aspx.

saving of a life to take precedence over observance of the law.[5] Your group might explore how these practices influence this story. Why would the disciples break the rule against reaping on the Sabbath simply because they are hungry? Why would Jesus defend them? What does this imply about what Jesus is teaching them? However, as always, don't force this conversation if it doesn't evolve naturally from your discussion.

For more background on Jesus' words about David eating the "holy bread," you could read the account in 1 Samuel 21:2-7.

St. Ignatius of Loyola was born in 1491. An expert in spiritual direction, Ignatius created *The Spiritual Exercises*, a compilation of prayers, meditations, and contemplative practices. With a small group of friends, he founded a religious community of priests called the Society of Jesus, also known as the Jesuits.(For more about his autobiography, see Appendix B, "A Guide to Reading Scripture, the Saints, and Spiritual Teachers" on page 101.)

St. Ignatius placed great emphasis on the power of the imagination in prayer. Ignatian contemplation involves placing yourself in a Gospel scene and imagining with your senses what it might look, smell, and feel like. This kind of imaginative prayer "seeks the truth of the heart rather than the truth of facts. The person who prays this way notices the feelings and desires inspired by an encounter with Jesus. To deepen the encounter, Ignatius recommends savoring the experience, returning to it again and again to relish the details . . . [Its] purpose is to call forth a heartfelt desire to know Jesus and to follow him."[6]

To learn more about Ignatian prayer and spirituality, visit the website Ignatian Spirituality at www.ignatianspirituality.com.

---

[5] Raymond E. Brown, SS; Joseph A. Fitzmyer, SJ; and Roland E. Murphy, OCarm, editors. "Matthew." *The New Jerome Biblical Commentary* (Englewood Cliffs: NJ: Prentice Hall, 1968, 1990), 653–654.

[6] "Ignatian Prayer and the Imagination." Online at the website Ignatian Spirituality, © 2009–2015 Loyola Press. Accessed at http://www.ignatianspirituality. com/ignatian-prayer/the-spiritual-exercises/ignatian-prayer-and-the-imagination.

Week 5
A Rich Young Man

As you review the recommended exercises, be sure to point your small group members to Appendix C, "A Guide to the Sacrament of Reconciliation" on page 102. If you're able to give a brief testimony to your own experience of Confession, do so. This could inspire others to receive this sacrament. Offer to share more of your experience with any of your group members individually if they are interested. You might also want to describe any prayers, examinations of conscience, or other methods of preparation that you have found helpful.

If someone in your group wants to learn more about the Sacrament of Reconciliation, suggest an accessible book, such as *7 Secrets of Confession* by Vinny Flynn (Ignatius Press, 2013). Flynn provides a relatable and refreshing perspective on Confession as a personal encounter with a Father who loves us. God our Father not only wants to forgive us but to restore and heal us as well. Read it first, though! *Only recommend a book that has helped you.* That way, you will know if it could bless the person to whom you recommend it.

Jesus looked at the rich young man and loved him. He looks at us with this same love. God's love gives us the courage to admit our sinfulness and ask for forgiveness.

The rich young man could not follow Christ fully because of his many possessions. All of us have at least one area preventing us from fully following Jesus. Pray for one another to recognize and turn away from these areas, and perhaps seek God's power and grace in the Sacrament of Reconciliation. In your discussion, some members may feel uncomfortable sharing their own personal weaknesses with the group. This is fine. Encourage them to bring those areas to the Lord in their own prayer, and remind them that our Lord doesn't want anyone to "go away sad" like the rich young man.

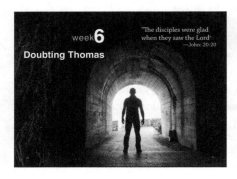

Week 6
Doubting Thomas

Week 6 includes both an "Encountering Christ This Week" and an "Encountering Christ for Life" section to conclude your small group. Ask the group in advance if they're willing to spend an extra fifteen or twenty minutes on this last session. The material in this extra section will help them apply the gifts and revelations they've received in this small group to their everyday lives. If adding time is not possible, skip the "Encountering Christ This Week" section in order to end at the same time while still discussing how to go forward.

If you skip "Encountering Christ This Week," summarize its content and strongly encourage everyone to meet with someone who, like Thomas, believes Jesus is Lord. This is a great way for all group members to extend their conversations about Jesus beyond the small group and to make or deepen Christian friendships.

Your group may decide that they want to continue meeting. That would be a gift from God and a tribute to your ability to facilitate well and create a loving community! The Evangelical Catholic has other small group guides that you could use for discussion (see our website, evangelicalcatholic.org), as do many other organizations.

Your group could study the Sunday Mass readings or read through a particular book of the Bible together. If you decide to explore the Bible, you can find many books and online resources on how to ask questions of the text that lead to fruitful discussion. The United States Conference of Catholic Bishops has excellent principles and resources for reading the Bible on its website (see usccb. org/bible/understanding-the-bible/index.cfm).

Whether or not you continue meeting, thank the group for the time they have given to it and the commitment they have shown. It's a great honor to walk with people on their spiritual journeys. Share that sentiment if you are moved to do so.

Try to have a more celebratory atmosphere at this last session by providing a dessert or another treat during the social time. You could ask members to bring something to share.

Appendix

Opening Prayer

We have provided a guided opening prayer for each session because it can help people who are completely new to small groups and shared extemporaneous prayer feel more at ease. If everyone or most people present are already comfortable speaking to God in their own words aloud in a group, you won't need these prayers at all. It's always better to talk to God from our hearts in small group. It contributes to the intimacy of the group and also builds individual intimacy with God.

Since some people have never witnessed spontaneous prayer, it's part of your role to model it. Prayers from the heart spoken aloud demonstrate how to talk to God honestly and openly. Seeing someone pray this way expands a person's understanding of who God is and the relationship they can have with Jesus Christ.

You can grow in extemporaneous prayer by praying aloud directly to Jesus during your personal prayer time and as you prepare for the group. This will help "prime the pump," so to speak.

Even if you enjoy praying spontaneously aloud, your goal as a facilitator is to provide opportunities for everyone to grow spiritually. People who pray aloud with others grow in leaps and bounds—we've seen it! After the first meeting, tell the group that you will allow time at the end of your extemporaneous prayer for others to voice prayers. As soon as the group appears to have grown into this, invite other people to open the group with prayer instead of leading it yourself or using the prayer provided.

If you don't do it in the first meeting, in the second week, pray the opening prayer in your own words. Here are some simple parts to include:

1. Praise God! Say what a great and wonderful God our Father is. Borrow language from the psalms of praise if you don't have your own. Just search online for "praise psalms."

2. Thank God! Thank the Lord for the gift of gathering together. Thank him for giving each person present the desire to sacrifice their time to attend the group. Thank him for the blessing of your parish or campus community.

3. Ask God for your needs. Ask God to bless your time together and to make it fruitful for all present as well as for his kingdom. Ask Jesus to be with you, who are two or three gathered in his name. Ask the Holy Spirit to open hearts, illuminate minds, and deepen each person's experience of Lent through the Scripture passages you'll read and discuss. Ask the Holy Spirit to guide the discussion so that you can all grow from it.

4. Close by invoking Jesus: "We pray this through Christ our Lord" or "We pray this in Jesus' name."

5. End with the Sign of the Cross.

Some essentials for extemporaneous prayer:

- Speak in the first-person plural "we." For example, "Holy Spirit, we ask you to open our hearts . . . " It's fine to add a line asking the Holy Spirit to help you facilitate the discussion as he wills, or something else to that effect, but most of the prayer should be for the whole group.

- Model speaking directly to Jesus our Lord. This may sound obvious, but among Catholic laypeople, it isn't frequently practiced or modeled. This is a very evangelical thing to do in the sense that it witnesses to the gospel. Not only does it show how much we believe that the Lord loves us, but it also demonstrates our confidence that Jesus himself is listening to us! As we say our Lord's name, we remind ourselves, as well as those who hear us, that we aren't just talking to ourselves. This builds up faith.

You and anyone unaccustomed to hearing someone pray to Jesus directly may feel a bit uncomfortable at first. But group members will quickly become more at ease as they hear these prayers repeatedly and experience more intimacy with Jesus. Bear in mind always that many graces come from praying "the name which is above every name" (Philippians 2:9).

If you've never publicly prayed to Jesus, you may feel childish at first, but pray for the humility of a child. After all, Jesus did say that we needed to become like children (Matthew18:3)! The more we pray directly to Jesus in our personal prayer, the less awkward it will feel when we pray to him publicly.

- Model great faith and trust that the Lord hears your prayer and will answer it. It's terrific just to say in prayer, "Jesus, we trust you!"

- You can always close extemporaneous prayer by inviting the whole group to join in a prayer of the Church, such as the Glory Be, the Our Father, or the Hail Mary. This will bring all into the prayer if previously, just one person was praying aloud extemporaneously.

Closing Prayer

For the closing prayer, we recommend that you always include extemporaneous prayer, even if you also use the prayer provided. No written prayer can address the thoughts, concerns, feelings, and inspirations that come up during the discussion.

If some group members already feel comfortable praying aloud in their own words, invite the group to join in the closing prayer right away. If not, wait a week or two. Once you feel that the group has the familiarity to prevent this from being too awkward, invite them to participate. You could tell the group that you will begin the closing prayer and then allow for a time of silence so that they can also pray aloud. Make sure they know that you will close the group's prayer by leading them into an Our Father after everyone is done praying spontaneously. This structure helps people feel that the time is contained and not completely lacking in structure. That helps free them to pray aloud.

Below are some possible ways to introduce your group to oral extemporaneous prayer. Don't read these suggestions verbatim—put them into your own words. It's not conducive to helping people become comfortable praying aloud spontaneously if you are reading out of a book!

"The closing prayer is a great time to take the reflections we've shared, bring them to God, and ask him to help us make any inspirations a reality in our lives. God doesn't care about how well-spoken or articulate we are when we pray, so we shouldn't either! We don't judge each other's prayers. Let's just pray from our hearts, knowing that God hears and cares about what we say, not how perfectly we say it. When we pray something aloud, we know that the Holy Spirit is mightily at work within us because it's the Spirit who gives us the courage to speak."

"Tonight for the closing prayer, let's first each voice our needs to one another; then we will take turns putting our right hand on the shoulder of the person to the right of us and praying for that person. After we each express our prayer needs, I will start by praying for Karen on my right. That means that I need to listen carefully when she tells us what she needs prayer for. We may not remember everyone's needs, so be sure to listen well to the person on your right. I'll voice my prayer needs first; then we'll go around the circle to the right. Then I will begin with the Sign of the Cross, and pray for _____ (name of person to the right) with my hand on her/his shoulder. Okay? Does anyone have any questions?"

Encountering Christ This Week

These weekly prayer and reflection exercises allow Jesus to enter more fully into the hearts of you and your small group members. If we don't give God the time that allows him to work in us, we experience far less fruit from our small group discussions. Prayer and reflection water the seeds that have been planted during the small group so they can take root. Without the "water" of prayer and reflection, the sun will scorch the seed, and it will shrivel up and die, "since it had no root" (Mark 4:6). Encountering Christ during the week on our own makes it possible for us to be "rooted in Christ" (cf. Colossians 2:7) and to drink deeply of the "living water" (John 4:10) that he longs to pour into our souls.

Please review the "Encountering Christ This Week" section in advance so that you're familiar with it, and then together as a group during each meeting. Reviewing it together will show everyone that it is an important part of the small group. Ask for feedback each week about how these prayer and reflection exercises are going. Don't spend too long on this topic, however, especially in the early weeks while members are still becoming comfortable together and growing more accustomed to praying on their own. Asking about their experience with the recommended prayer, sacrament, or spiritual exercise will help you know who is hungry for spiritual growth and who might need more encouragement. The witness of participants' stories from their times of prayer can ignite the interest of others who are less motivated to pray.

About The Evangelical Catholic

The Evangelical Catholic (EC) equips Catholic ministries for evangelization by inspiring, training, and supporting local leaders to launch dynamic outreach. Through training events, services, and ongoing contractual relationships, the EC forms and trains Catholic pastoral staff and lay leaders for long-term evangelical efforts that can be locally sustained without ongoing site visits and regular consulting.

To accomplish this mission, we equip the lay faithful to invite the lost into the joy of life in Christ and stem the tide of Catholics leaving the Church. We form pastoral staff to make disciples, shepherd evangelistic ministries, and manage pastoral structure to make discipleship to Jesus the natural outcome within the parish or university campus ministry.

Our prayer is that through the grace of the Holy Spirit, we can help make the Church's mission of evangelization accessible, natural, and fruitful for every Catholic, and that many lives will be healed and transformed by knowing Jesus within the Church.